RECORD-BREAKING PEOPLE

Jon Richards
and Ed Simkins

HUNGRY
TOMATO™

MINNEAPOLIS

CONTENTS

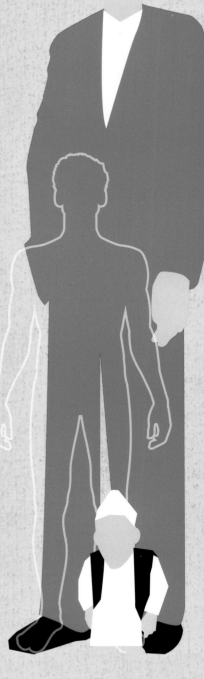

4 **Super Cells**

6 Organs and Systems

8 **Body Extremes**

10 Living Long

12 **On the Run**

14 Throwing and Jumping

16 **Swimming and Diving**

18 Superstrong

20 **The Silver Screen**

22 That's Rich!

24 **Works of Art**

26 Tune Time

28 **Best Sellers**

30 Glossary

31 Websites

32 Index

pages 8–9
Meet the tallest and shortest people and compare your hand to the biggest in the world.

WELCOME!

From the tallest to the shortest, the fastest to the strongest, and the oldest to the richest, this book looks at amazing human record-breakers. It uses stunning icons, graphics, and visualizations to show you how people keep pushing their potential to the absolute limits.

pages 16–17
See just how far some divers can swim underwater on a single breath of air.

pages 20–21
Compare the size of the largest movie cast with the population of Iceland.

pages 28–29
Measure the world's largest book next to a giraffe.

SUPER CELLS

The trillions of cells in your body come in all shapes and sizes. The largest are just visible to the naked eye, while the longest stretch the whole length of your legs. Together, these amazing cells create tissues that form the building blocks of your body.

The largest human cell is the egg, or ovum. One of these can measure about 0.04 inches (1 millimeter) across. The smallest cell is the sperm, which measures about **0.002 inches (0.06 mm)** long—about 10 could fit on the period at the end of this sentence.

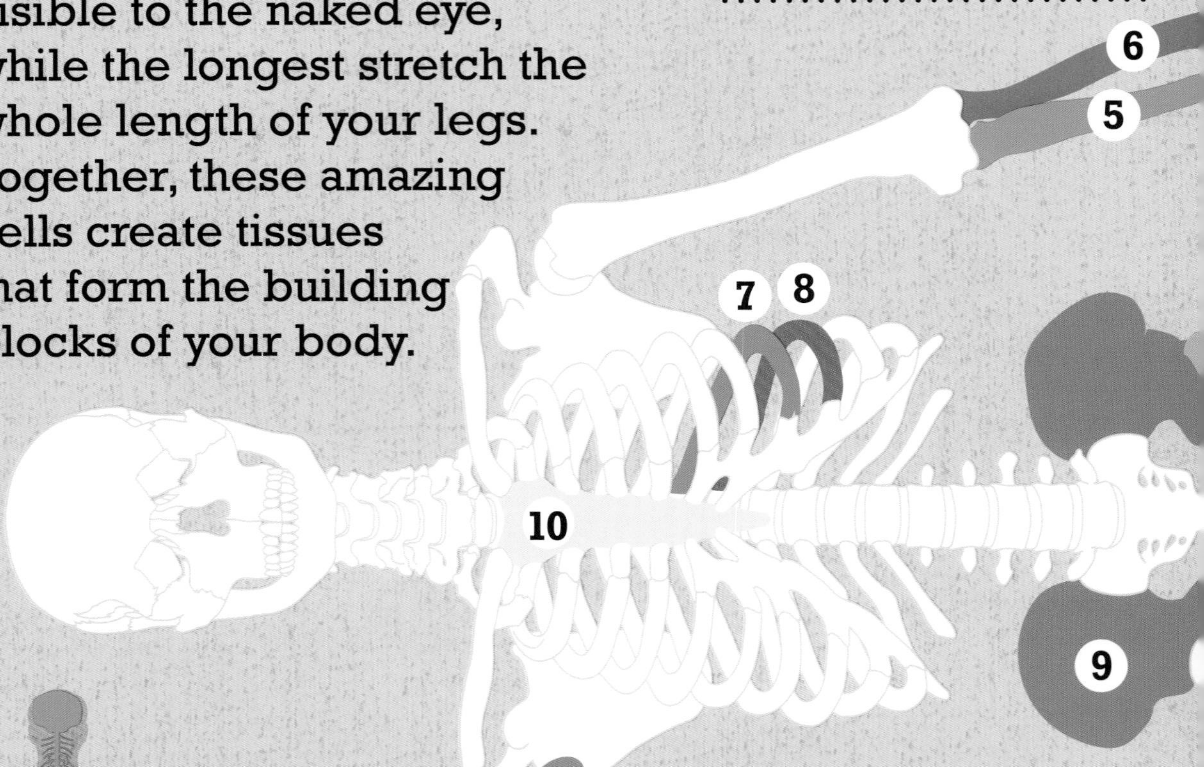

6

5

7 **8**

10

9

4

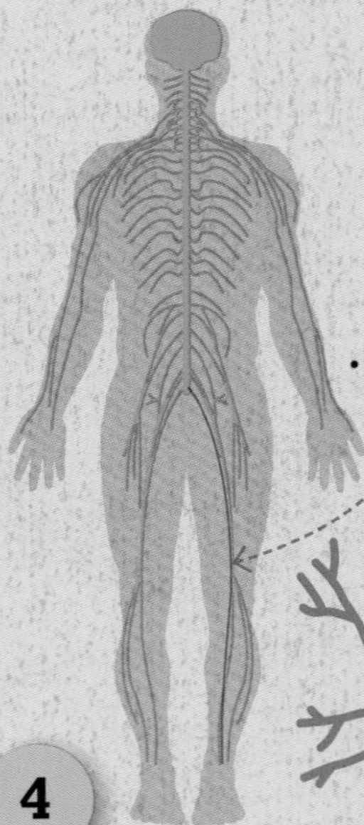

motor neuron

The **longest cells** in the human body are motor neurons that stretch from the base of the **spine** to the muscles in the **toes**.

Longest cell

They can be up to 3.3 feet (1 meter) long.

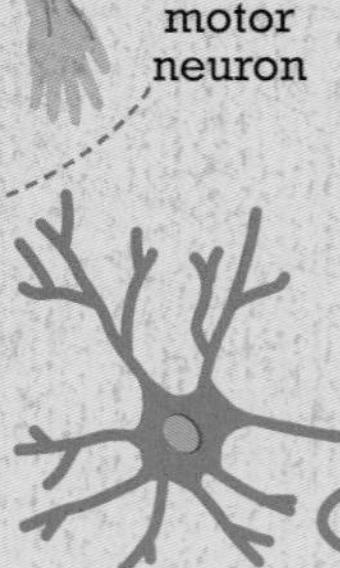

4

Magnified × 70

egg

sperm

LONGEST BONES IN THE HUMAN BODY
AVERAGE LENGTH—INCHES (CENTIMETERS)

1. **Femur (thighbone)—19.9 (50.5)**
2. **Tibia (shinbone)—16.9 (42.9)**
3. **Fibula (lower leg)—15.9 (40.4)**
4. **Humerus (upper arm)—14.4 (36.6)**
5. **Ulna (inner lower arm)—11.1 (28.2)**
6. **Radius (outer lower arm)—10.3 (26.4)**
7. **Seventh rib—9.6 (24.4)**
8. **Eighth rib—9.1 (23.1)**
9. **Innominate bone (hip bone)—7.3 (18.5)**
10. **Sternum (breastbone)—6.7 (17)**

1

2

3

Long legs

The leg of an adult human is just under **3.3 feet (1 m)** long.

In comparison, a giraffe's leg is nearly twice as long, about 5.9 feet (1.8 m) long.

40%
Skeletal muscle makes up about 40 percent of your body's mass.

In an adult weighing 154 pounds (70 kilograms), that means **62 pounds (28 kilograms)** is muscle, which is more than the weight of **two gold bars**.

Muscle tissue

ORGANS AND SYSTEMS

<‹ ·················· ›>

The largest, heaviest organ in your body covers you completely, protecting you from the outside world. Your other organs perform an amazing range of tasks, allowing you to live, grow, and survive.

Brain bits

The cerebrum is the upper portion of the brain and is its largest part, making up about…

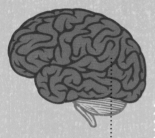

…85% of the brain's mass.

The brain is the fattest organ in the human body.

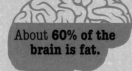

About **60%** of the brain is fat.

9 Thyroid
This butterfly-shaped organ is found in your neck and produces several chemicals that tell your body how to behave.

1.2 ounces (35 grams)

4 Lungs
These large sacs fill with air when you breathe in so that oxygen passes into your body and carbon dioxide passes out.

38.4 ounces (1,090 g)

3 Brain
Protected by your skull, this organ receives signals from all over your body and weighs as much as two basketballs.

44.6 ounces (1,263 g)

5 Heart
This muscular organ is part of the blood, or circulatory, system. It weighs a little less than a tin of soup.

11.1 ounces (315 g)

Thick-skinned

Skin is usually 0.04 to 0.08 inches (1 to 2 mm) thick. Your eyelids are only about 0.02 inches (0.5 mm) thick, while parts of your upper back have skin that is 0.2 inches (5 mm) thick.

0.04 to 0.08 inches

0.02 inches

0.2 inches

Your body has about **1.5 gallons of blood**, equivalent to 5.6 one-liter bottles. This blood is pushed by the heart through the body **three times every minute**.

In one day, the blood travels a total of **11,806 miles (19,000 kilometers)**—that is four times the distance across the **United States**, from coast to coast.

4

Blood system facts

7 ### Spleen
This organ acts as a blood reserve. It also removes old red blood cells and helps the immune system.

6 ounces (170 g)

8 ### Pancreas
This organ produces chemicals that tell your body how to act, as well as enzymes, which break down food.

3.5 ounces (98 g)

Your stomach
is a stretchy bag of muscle that gets bigger and smaller as food enters and leaves it. An adult stomach can expand to hold up to 0.4 gallons (1.5 liters) of food.

1 ### Skin
This organ covers your entire body and prevents water loss. It weighs about as much as four bricks.

384 ounces (10,886 g)

6 ### Kidneys
These two organs lie on either side of your back. They filter your blood, removing harmful waste products.

10.2 ounces (290 g)

2 ### Liver
Part of your digestive system, this organ helps you to break down and process what you eat.

55 ounces (1,560 g)

10 ### Prostate
This small, walnut-size male organ makes seminal fluid, which sperm cells travel in.

0.7 ounces (20 g)

BODY EXTREMES

Growing the longest body parts can take decades of dedicated care and attention. Other body part records, however, come a little more naturally.

1 Longest hair

Xie Qiuping of China has been growing her hair for more than 40 years. It is nearly three times as long as a bed.

18.4 feet (5.6 m)

2 Longest nails

Lee Redmond of the United States spent nearly 30 years growing and looking after her nails.

28.5 feet (8.7 m) (total length)

3 Longest nose

When measured from the bridge of the nose to its tip, Mehmet Ozyurek of Turkey has the longest nose of any living person.

3.5 inches (8.8 cm)

Life size!

4 Longest mustache

Ram Singh Chauhan of India grew a mustache that was longer than a Volkswagen Beetle.

14.1 feet (4.3 m)

77.2 inches (196 cm)

52 inches (132 cm)

5 Longest legs

Svetlana Pankratova from Russia holds the record for the world's longest legs. They make up more than two-thirds of her total height!

52 inches (132 cm)

Most fingers and toes

Akshat Saxena from India was born with a condition called polydactylism—he had more fingers and toes than normal.

14 fingers (7 on each hand)
20 toes (10 on each foot)

6

7 Largest hands

Robert Wadlow of Illinois had hands that measured 12.7 inches (32.3 cm) from the wrist to the tip of the middle finger.

12.7 inches (32.3 cm)

8 Largest feet

He also had the largest feet ever measured. They were 19 inches (47 cm) long!

Size 37AA

5-foot-9-inch tall (1.8 m) man

Robert Waldow's shoe size

average men's shoe size (size 10)

9 Tallest person

In fact, Robert Wadlow holds the record as the tallest person who has ever lived.

8.9 feet (2.7 m)

10 Shortest person

In contrast, Chandra Bahadur Dangi from Nepal is the shortest living person and is only one-fifth of Wadlow's height.

21.5 inches (54.6 cm)

LIVING LONG

With improvements in medicine and diet, it is not uncommon for someone in a rich country to live 100 years or more. However, there are still many poor countries where people have low life expectancy.

Growing old

By 2050, studies predict that there will be **1.56 billion** people over the age of **65**, making up about **17 percent** of the world's population.

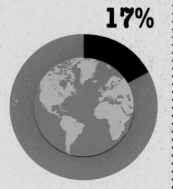

17%

1.56 billion

Aging Americans

By 2050, the number of people over 65 in the United States will **more than double**. It is predicted that the number of people aged **over 100** will soar from 72,000 in 2000 to 834,000.

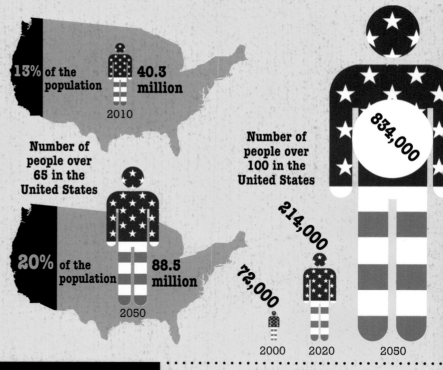

13% of the population — **40.3 million** — 2010

Number of people over 65 in the United States

20% of the population — **88.5 million** — 2050

Number of people over 100 in the United States

834,000

214,000

72,000

2000   2020   2050

Oldest person who's ever lived

Born February 21, 1875

Jeanne Louise Calment from France lived for 122 years and 164 days, from February 21, 1875, to August 4, 1997.

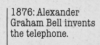

1876: Alexander Graham Bell invents the telephone.

1903: The Wright brothers make the first powered flight at Kitty Hawk, North Carolina.

1928: The first transatlantic television signal is sent between London and New York.

1875   1885   1895   1905   1915   1925

Lowest life expectancy

PLACES WHERE PEOPLE LIVE THE LONGEST
(LIFE EXPECTANCY—YEARS)

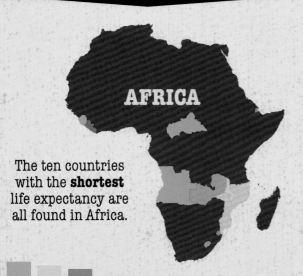

AFRICA

The ten countries with the **shortest** life expectancy are all found in Africa.

1.	Switzerland—82.70
2.	Japan—82.59
3.	Iceland—82.36
4.	Spain—82.33
5.	Italy—82.09
6.	Australia—81.85
7.	Sweden—81.80
8.	Israel—81.76
9	France—81.67
10.	Norway—81.30

Central African Republic—44.5 years

Malawi—43.8 years

Djibouti—43.4 years

Liberia—41.8 years

Sierra Leone—41.2 years

Mozambique—41.2 years

Lesotho—40.4 years

Zambia—38.6 years

Angola—38.2 years

Swaziland—31.9 years

1900   2000

A Swiss man born in 1900 had a life expectancy of **51**. One born in 2000 can expect to live to **85**. By 2050, some studies show that **2.2 million** Swiss, nearly **30 percent**, will be older than 65.

Aging Swiss

1010
0101

1938: The world's first freely programmable computer, the Z1, is built by Konrad Zuse.

1961: Yuri Gagarin becomes the first person to orbit Earth.

1969: the Apollo 11 mission lands the first people on the moon.

1978: Louise Brown, the world's first test tube baby, is born.

Dies August 4, 1997

1945   1955   1965   1975   1985   1995

ON THE RUN

The world's fastest sprinters can run at 28 miles (45 km) per hour, but they can only manage this pace for a short time. Other runners need more endurance than speed to cross deserts or climb skyscrapers during some races.

In just **four years**, two Jamaican sprinters managed to set **five** new world 100-meter records.

August 16, 2009
August 16, 2008
May 31, 2008
September 9, 2007
June 14, 2005

| 9.5 | 9.6 | 9.7 | 9.8 | 9.9 | 10 |

9.58 seconds
9.69 seconds
9.72 seconds
9.74 seconds
9.77 seconds

← - - - - - - - Usain Bolt - - - - - - - - - → ← - - - - Asafa Powell - - - - →

How far in 10 seconds?

These bars show the distance a sprinter, a marathon runner, a record-breaking swimmer, and a person moving at normal walking pace could cover in 10 seconds.

Olympic sprinter—328 feet (100 m)
Marathon runner—187.7 feet (57.2 m)
Olympic swimmer—78.7 feet (24 m)
Walking pace—52.5 feet (16 m)

← - - - - - - - - - - - - - - - - - - **10 seconds** - - - - - - - - - - - - - - - →

RUNNING RECORDS

1. **100 meters: Usain Bolt (Jamaica)—9.58 secs.**

2. 110-meter hurdles: Aries Merritt (USA)—12.8 secs.

3. **200 meters: Usain Bolt (Jamaica)—19.19 secs.**

4. 400 meters: Michael Johnson (USA)—43.18 secs.

5. **800 meters: David Lekuta Rudisha (Kenya)—1 min., 40.91 secs.**

6. 1,500 meters: Hicham El Guerrouj (Morocco)—3 mins., 26 secs.

7. **5,000 meters: Kenenisa Bekele (Ethiopia)—12 mins., 37.35 secs.**

8. 10,000 meters: Kenenisa Bekele (Ethiopia)—26 mins., 17.53 secs.

9. **Half marathon: Zersenay Tadese (Eritrea)—58 mins., 23 secs.**

10. Marathon: Dennis Kimetto (Kenya)—2 hrs., 2 mins., 57 secs.

Ultramarathon

Ultramarathon runner Marshall Ulrich ran **3,063 miles (4,930 km)** from San Francisco to New York in just **52 days**. That is nearly **59 miles (95 km)** every day!

San Francisco

New York

At the
1896 Olympic Games
in Athens, Spiridon Louis of Greece won the gold medal in the marathon, completing the race in a time of 2 hours, 58 minutes, 50 seconds.

86th floor

1,050 feet (320 m)

MARATHON DES SABLES

Competitors in the Marathon des Sables have to run 156 miles (251 km) across the northern African desert in six days, experiencing temperatures over 122°F (50°C).

Empire State Building

Every year, more than **400 athletes** race up the Empire State Building in New York City. They run up to the **86th floor**, climbing **1,576 steps** on the way. The winner usually completes the race in a little over **10 minutes**.

THROWING AND JUMPING

Power, speed, and agility are vital to smash throwing and jumping records. Throwers will try to go farther than anyone before, while jumpers will go for distance and height to become world record holders.

Standing jumps

The **standing** high jump and long jump appeared at the Olympic Games until 1912. Athletes tried to jump as **high** or as **long** as they could from a standing start. Today, competitors take a **running jump**.

Record distance—12.17 feet (3.71 m)

Standing long jump

Record height—4.86 feet (1.48 m)

Standing high jump

Throwing records

GRAPE THROW AND CATCH
A. J. Henderson managed to throw a **grape**, run, and catch it in his mouth over a distance of 69.5 feet (21.18 m), which is about the length of two buses.

LIGHTBULB
A **lightbulb** was thrown for a record 106.73 feet (32.53 m) by Bipin Larkin.

33 feet (10 m)

0 feet

THROWING AND JUMPING RECORDS

1. **Javelin:** Jan Zelezny (Czech Republic), May 25, 1996—323.1 feet (98.48 m)

2. **Discus:** Jürgen Schult (East Germany), June 6, 1986—243.04 feet (74.08 m)

3. **Hammer:** Yuriy Sedykh (USSR), August 30, 1986—284.58 feet (86.74 m)

4. **Shot put:** Randy Barnes (USA), May 20, 1990—75.85 feet (23.12 m)

5. **Long jump:** Mike Powell (USA), August 30, 1991—29.36 feet (8.95 m)

6. **Pole vault:** Renaud Lavillenie (France), February 15, 2014—20.21 feet (6.16 m)

7. **Triple jump:** Jonathan Edwards (UK), August 7, 1995—60 feet (18.29 m)

8. **Standing high jump:** Jonas Huusom (Denmark), August 27, 2011—4.86 feet (1.48 m)

9. **High jump:** Javier Sotomayor (Cuba), July 27, 1993—8.04 feet (2.45 m)

10. **Standing long jump:** Arne Tvervaag (Norway), November 11, 1968—12.17 feet (3.71 m)

High jump styles

Over the years, athletes have used and developed different high jump styles. Today's jumpers use the **Fosbury flop**, developed by Dick Fosbury in 1965.

scissors

straddle

western roll

Fosbury flop

LONGEST PEANUT THROW
Former world champion hurdler Colin Jackson holds the record for the longest **peanut** throw, at 124.41 feet (37.92 m).

EGG THROW AND CATCH
This record is held by Willie O'Donevan and Warren McElhone and stands at 233.6 feet (71.2 m).

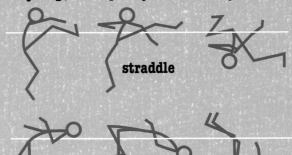

230 feet (70 m)

SWIMMING AND DIVING

Take a deep breath and plunge beneath the surface with these amazing water sports records. They can involve diving from a great height, plunging to the ocean's depths, or racing through a swimming pool.

Free diving

<- 328 feet (100 m) ->

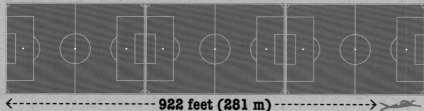

<- 922 feet (281 m) ->

Dynamic apnea with fins involves swimming as far as possible **underwater** on one breath. The record is held by Goran Colak from Croatia, and it is **922 feet (281 m)**— that's nearly three soccer fields.

Deepest dive

Herbert Nitsch of Austria dived to a depth of **702 feet (214 m)** and returned to the surface on a single breath! That's more than twice the height of the **Statue of Liberty**.

702 feet (214 m)

305 feet (93 m)

Diving

Cliff divers jump off a platform that's 89 feet (27 m) above the water—as tall as a nine-story building.

89 feet (27 m)

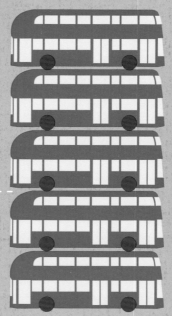

The highest board at an indoor diving competition is 33 feet (10 m) high— **twice the height of a double-decker bus**.

SWIMMING RECORDS

1. **50 m freestyle:** Cesar Cielo (Brazil)—20.91 secs.

2. **50 m breaststroke:** Cameron van der Burgh (South Africa)—26.67 secs.

3. **50 m backstroke:** Liam Tancock (UK)—24.04 secs.

4. **50 m butterfly:** Rafael Munoz (Spain)—22.43 secs.

5. **100 m freestyle:** Cesar Cielo (Brazil)—46.91 secs.

6. **100 m breaststroke:** Cameron van der Burgh (South Africa)—58.46 secs.

7. **100 m backstroke:** Aaron Peirsol (USA)—51.94 secs.

8. **100 m butterfly:** Michael Phelps (USA)—49.82 secs.

9. **4 x 100 m freestyle:** USA—3 mins., 8.24 secs.

10. **4 x 100 m medley:** USA—3 mins., 27.28 secs.

Longest unassisted swim

Chloe McCardel of Australia swam for **42 hours** and covered **78 miles (126 km)**—more than **four times** the distance across the English Channel.

78 miles
(126 km)
in 42 hours

Swimming strokes

There are four types of **strokes** used at swimming competitions: freestyle (or front crawl), backstroke, breaststroke, and butterfly. **Medleys** are a special type of race where swimmers use all four styles, one after the other.

freestyle

backstroke

breaststroke

butterfly

SUPERSTRONG

These people are the strongest on the planet! They can lift, pull, and carry enormous weights many times their own body weight and regularly take part in competitions to see who is the strongest.

Weight-lifting techniques

Breaking **powerlifting** and **weight-lifting** records involves trying to lift as much as possible using the techniques shown here.

snatch

clean and jerk

dead lift

squat

bench press

Dariusz Slowik from Poland threw a **106-pound (48 kg)** washing machine a distance of **11.5 feet (3.5 m)** to set a new record.

Lance Karabel of the United States holds the record for the squat, carrying 1,003 pounds (455 kg)—that's almost the same as the weight of an adult male grizzly bear.

POWERLIFTING & WEIGHT-LIFTING RECORDS

1. **Snatch (men): Behdad Salimkordasiabi (Iran)**—472 pounds (214 kg)

2. **Clean and jerk (men): Hossein Rezazadeh (Iran)**—580 pounds (263 kg)

3. **Combined snatch and clean and jerk (men): Hossein Rezazadeh (Iran)**— 1,041 pounds (472 kg)

4. **Snatch (women): Tatiana Kashirina (Russia)**—333 pounds (151 kg)

5. **Clean and jerk (women): Tatiana Kashirina (Russia)**—419 pounds (190 kg)

6. **Combined snatch and clean and jerk (women): Tatiana Kashirina (Russia)**—736 pounds (334 kg)

7. **Squat: Lance Karabel (USA)**—1,003 pounds (455 kg)

8. **Bench press: Allen Baria (USA)**—854.3 pounds (387.5 kg)

9. **Dead lift: Vugar Namazov (Azerbaijan)**—370 pounds (816 kg)

10. **Combined squat, bench press, and dead lift: Lance Karabel (USA)**—2,414 pounds (1,095 kg)

World's strongest

Mariusz Pudzianowski of Poland has won the World's Strongest Man competition five times. Aneta Florczyk, also of Poland, holds the women's record with four wins. Here are some of the events that competitors take part in.

overhead log lift

farmer's walk

Atlas stones

vehicle pull

The Reverend Kevin Fast from Canada lifted 22 people who were standing on a platform.

Manjit Singh

Manjit Singh of the United Kingdom pulled a bus weighing **17,637 pounds (8,000 kg)** using ribbons tied to his hair. That's about the same weight as 1.5 elephants.

He holds more than **30 strength records**, including pulling a bus with **54 people** on board with one hand.

He also pulled a **Vulcan jet bomber** weighing in at **202,825 pounds (92,000 kg)** a distance of **6 inches (15 cm)** using a harness.

THE SILVER SCREEN

Lights, camera, action! Since the first movies were made at the end of the 19th century, people have been producing films that continue to set records for money earned, number of people appearing, size, and endurance!

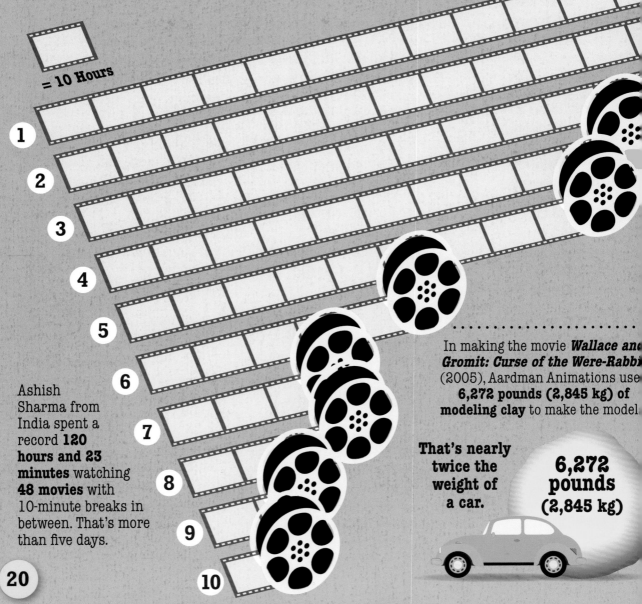

= 10 Hours

1

2

3

4

5

6

7

8

9

10

Ashish Sharma from India spent a record **120 hours and 23 minutes** watching **48 movies** with 10-minute breaks in between. That's more than five days.

In making the movie **Wallace and Gromit: Curse of the Were-Rabbit** (2005), Aardman Animations used **6,272 pounds (2,845 kg) of modeling clay** to make the model.

That's nearly twice the weight of a car.

6,272 pounds (2,845 kg)

GONE WITH THE WIND

CLARK GABLE
VIVIEN LEIGH
LESLIE HOWARD OLIVIA DE HAVILLAND

Highest-grossing film

When adjusted for inflation, the highest-grossing movie of all time is *Gone with the Wind*. Its adjusted figure comes in at **$5.3 billion.** In contrast, *Avatar* (2009), which holds the record for the highest-grossing movie (unadjusted), took in **$2.8 billion.**

Tiniest film

Measuring just **45 by 25 nanometers**, a 60-second stop-motion film made by IBM is the smallest movie ever made. It was made using individual molecules, placing and moving them for each shot. The film tells the story of a boy playing with a ball.

Largest cast

More than **300,000 actors and extras** appeared in one scene for the movie *Gandhi* (1982). That is nearly the same size as the entire population of Iceland.

LONGEST FILMS EVER MADE

1. *Modern Times Forever* (2011)—**14,400 minutes (240 hours, or 10 days)**

2. *Cinématon* (1984)—11,220 minutes (187 hours, or 7 days, 19 hours)

3. *Beijing 2003* (2004)—**9,000 minutes (150 hours, or 6 days, 6 hours)**

4. *Matrjoschka* (2006)—5,700 minutes (95 hours, or 3 days 23 hours)

5. *The Cure for Insomnia* (1987)—**5,220 minutes (87 hours, or 3 days, 15 hours)**

6. *The Longest Most Meaningless Movie in the World* (1970)—2,880 minutes (48 hours)

7. ****** (1967)—**1,500 minutes (25 hours)**

8. *The Clock* (2010)—1,440 minutes (24 hours)

9. *A Journal of Crude Oil* (2008)—**840 minutes (14 hours)**

10. *Tie Xi Qu: West of the Tracks* (2003)—551 minutes (9 hours, 11 minutes)

THAT'S RICH!

These people are the richest on the planet. They have accumulated huge amounts of wealth in industries such as computer software, airlines, telecommunications, and investments.

North America

441

26%

Where do the billionaires live?

This map shows the **distribution** of the world's billionaires, with most living in **Europe and Asia** and the fewest found in **Australasia and Africa**.

Total number of billionaires **1,682**

6%

Latin America

94

RICHEST PEOPLE

1. **Bill Gates (USA)—$78.9 billion**

2. **Carlos Slim Helu (Mexico)—$78.8 billion**

3. **Warren Buffett (USA)—$66.1 billion**

4. **Amancio Ortega (Spain)—$55.1 billion**

5. **Larry Ellison (USA)—$47.1 billion**

6. **Charles Koch (USA)—$39.7 billion**

=6. **David Koch (USA)—$39.7 billion**

8. **Christy Walton (USA)—$36.9 billion**

9. **Jim Walton (USA)—$35.5 billion**

10. **Liliane Bettencourt (France)—$34.1 billion**

Bill Gates, the world's richest person, has given away more than $30 billion to charitable causes since 2000, through the Bill and Melinda Gates Foundation.

Richest city

The city with the most billionaires is Moscow. It has...

...**84** billionaires with a combined wealth of **$366 billion**.

This is enough wealth to purchase nearly **750,000 gold bars**.

It is also more than the gross domestic product (annual earnings) of South Africa.

Europe and Russia
505
30%

Moscow

29%

Asia
488

1.5%

Africa
25

Middle East
108

6.5%

Australasia
21

1%

Where can money take you?

The total combined wealth of the world's billionaires comes to **$6.4 trillion**.

Changed into quarters, this money would create a stack of coins **27.8 million miles (44.8 million kg) tall**. That's long enough to stretch nearly **1,120 times around the globe** or more than...

Enough to give everyone on the planet **more than $900**.

...**58 times to the moon and back.**

WORKS OF ART

These paintings were created by some of the best-known artists who ever lived. Although not all achieved success in their lifetimes, their works have gone on to sell for hundreds of millions of dollars.

1

1894–1895

2

1932

Least valuable art collection

The Museum of Bad Art in Boston holds the record for the least valuable art collection. Its 573 works are worth just $1,197.35, **or $2.09 each**.

3

1969

4

Vincent van Gogh produced more than **2,000** works of art, but he only sold **one** while he was alive.

1948

5

1953

6

1907

Oldest art

Made by Neanderthals around **40,000 years ago**, scratches found on a cave wall in Gibraltar may be Europe's oldest art.

MOST EXPENSIVE WORKS OF ART

1. *The Card Players*, Paul Cézanne—$259 million

2. *Le Rêve*, Pablo Picasso—$155 million

3. *Three Studies of Lucian Freud*, Francis Bacon—$142.4 million

4. *No. 5, 1948*, Jackson Pollock—$140 million

5. *Woman III*, Willem de Kooning—$137.5 million

6. *Portrait of Adele Bloch-Bauer I*, Gustav Klimt—$135 million

7. *The Scream*, Edvard Munch—$119.9 million

8. *Flag*, Jasper Johns—$110 million

9. *Nude, Green Leaves and Bust*, Pablo Picasso—$106 million

10. *Anna's Light*, Barnett Newman—$105.7 million

1893

1954–1955

1932

1968

Marree Man

This is the largest human art figure ever made. It was carved into the ground in Australia and measured 2.6 miles (4.2 km) long. It appeared in 1998 and could only be seen from the air. No one knows who made it or why.

2.6 miles (4.2 km)

Micro art

Willard Wigan from the United Kingdom creates microscopic sculptures. They are so small that they can sit inside the eye of a needle.

actual size

TUNE TIME

These artists are the top of the pop stars in the world! They've sold more songs and records than anyone else, had their songs played more times, had more No. 1s, and had longer recording careers than any other acts on the planet.

Top-selling artists (digital singles)

The best-selling digital single ever is **"I Gotta Feeling"** by the Black Eyed Peas. Released in 2009, the song has been downloaded more than eight million times.

Artist	Sales
Katy Perry	72 million
Taylor Swift	66.5 million
Rihanna	52 million
Kanye West	32.5 million
Lil Wayne	32 million

Most No.1 albums

Having sold more than 42 million copies since its release in 1982, *Thriller* by Michael Jackson is the best-selling album of all time.

10
Bruce Springsteen
Elvis Presley
Barbra Streisand

Most played tune

The Disney tune **"It's a Small World"** may be the most played tune in the world. It's more than 50 years old, and it is played continually at all the company's theme parks. It may have been played **more than 50 million times**.

During a 16-hour day, it's played 1,200 times.

Longest career

The record for the longest career as a recording artist belongs to Judy Robinson. She released her first record in **1926,** and her last recording was made in **2003.**

77 years

Fastest selling

278,000

Taylor Swift holds the record for the fastest-selling digital album in the United States. In **2010, it was downloaded 278,000 times** in just one week.

MOST SUCCESSFUL RECORDING ARTISTS OF ALL TIME
(WORLDWIDE SALES—IN MILLIONS)

1. **The Beatles—600**
2. **Elvis Presley—500 to 600**
3. **Michael Jackson—300 to 400**
4. **Madonna—275 to 300**
5. **Elton John—250 to 300**
6. **Led Zeppelin—300**
7. **Pink Floyd—200 to 250**
8. **Mariah Carey—175 to 200**
=8. **Celine Dione—175 to 200**
9. **Whitney Houston—170 to 200**
10. **AC/DC—150 to 200**

Most records

In 1975, the British rock band Led Zeppelin became the first band to have six albums on the charts at the same time.

13 Jay-Z

19 Beatles

Streaming music

Songs played on the Internet streaming services, such as Spotify, account for **more than one-quarter** of the music industry's earnings.

Record piano players

In 2012, the record for the greatest number of musicians playing a piano was set when 103 people took turns to play part of Beethoven's "Ode to Joy" at a concert in Japan.

BEST SELLERS

Every year, billions of books are bought and read either in printed form or on e-readers and tablets. The people on these pages knew what made a good read. Meet the most successful, most prolific, and biggest-selling authors of all time!

Shakespeare records

As well as being the world's best-selling author, William Shakespeare is believed to have invented, or introduced, more than **1,700 new words**.

His longest play, *Hamlet*, has 4,042 lines and 29,551 words. The character of Hamlet alone has 1,569 lines.

All of his works were recited over 110 hours in 1987 during the longest ever theater performance.

Most filmed author

420 films and TV movies

 Hamlet 79 movies

 **Romeo and Juliet** 52 movies

 Macbeth 36 movies

Largest book

The largest book in the world is **This the Prophet Mohamed**, published by the Mshahed International Group, Dubai.

It measures 16.4 feet by 26.44 feet (5 m by 8.06 m) and weighs 3,307 pounds (1,500 kg).

That's **taller than a giraffe** and weighs more than 20 adults, or **about the weight of a car**.

BEST-SELLING AUTHORS OF ALL TIME (ESTIMATED SALES)

1. **William Shakespeare—2 to 4.5 billion**
2. **Agatha Christie—2 to 4 billion**
3. **Barbara Cartland—0.5 to 1 billion**
=3. **Danielle Steel—0.5 to1 billion**
5. **Harold Robbins—800 million**
6. **Georges Simenon—500 to 800 million**
=6. **Charles Dickens—500 to 800 million**
8. **Sidney Sheldon—400 to 600 million**
9. **Enid Blyton—350 to 600 million**
10. **Robert Ludlum—300 to 500 million**

The Way to Happiness

by L. Ron Hubbard is the most translated book in the world. It can be read in 70 different languages, including Samoan and Uzbek.

Largest bookstore

The world's largest bookstore is Barnes & Noble in New York City. It covers **154,247 square feet (14,330 sq. m)**, the size of nearly **2.5 soccer fields**...

...and has **12.87 miles (20.71 km)** of shelves.

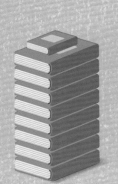

Lauran Bosworth Paine
1916–2001 **850 books**

Kathleen Lindsay
1903–1973 **904 books**

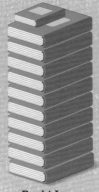

Ryoki Inoue
1946– **1,086 books**

Edward Stratemeyer
1862–1930 **1,300 books**

Corin Tellado
1927–2009
4,000 books

= 100 books

Most prolific writers

GLOSSARY

agility
to be able to move around, perform actions, and change the position and direction of the body easily

album
a collection of songs or music recordings

cells
the smallest parts of the body. There are many different types of cells, and they combine in different ways to form all the body's structures.

circulatory system
a collection of organs, tissues, and cells—including the heart and blood vessels—which helps to transport blood and the oxygen and nutrients it contains around the body

digestive system
a network of organs, tissues, and cells that work together to take in food, extract its nutrients, and expel any waste products

digital single
a song or a piece of music that exists only as a digital file that can be downloaded

dynamic apnea
a sport where people see how far they can swim underwater just by holding their breath and not by using any special breathing apparatus

endurance
the ability to withstand something, put up with something, or do something difficult for a long period of time

enzyme
a type of protein produced by the body that aids certain chemical reactions

e-reader
an electronic device for storing and displaying electronic written content, such as a book or a newspaper

gross domestic product
the total value of the amount of goods and services produced by a country during a year

immune system
a collection of organs, tissues, and cells that help to protect the body from infection and disease

inflation
the process of things becoming more expensive over time

life expectancy
the average age a person can expect to live to. It varies from country to country. Before the era of modern medicine, people had a much lower life expectancy.

motor neuron
a type of long cell that runs through the spine and carries messages to the body's muscles in the form of tiny electrical signals

nanometer
a tiny unit of measurement equal to just one billionth of a meter

organ
a part of the body that carries out certain tasks or functions. The brain, the heart, and the liver are all organs.

prolific
producing a lot of work

skeletal muscle
muscles that are attached to the skeleton and give the body its shape. They can be consciously controlled and moved via messages from the brain.

stop-motion film
a type of movie where models or objects are filmed and then moved, one frame at a time. When shown at normal speed, this makes it look as if the objects are moving on their own.

streaming
listening to or watching a digital file, such as a song or a film, over the Internet in real time

WEBSITES

◀ • ▶

BBC: Human Planet Explorer
http://www.bbc.co.uk/nature/humanplanetexplorer/
Discover incredible human stories from around the world.

Cool Infographics
http://www.coolinfographics.com
The site has infographics and data visualizations from online resources, magazines, and newspapers.

Daily Infographics
http://www.dailyinfographic.com
This comprehensive collection of infographics on an enormous range of topics is updated every day.

Data Visualization Encyclopedia
http://www.visualinformation.info
This website contains a whole host of infographic material on subjects as diverse as natural history, science, sports, and computer games.

Guiness World Records
http://www.guinessworldrecords.com
This website is about all things record-breaking. It is packed with thousands of world records and facts.

National Geographic: Human Body
http://science.nationalgeographic.com/science/health-and-human-body/human-body/
Get facts, photos, videos, games, and more about the human body.

INDEX

albums, **26–27**
art, **24–25**
authors, **28–29**

best-selling author, **28–29**
best-selling digital
    single, **26**
billionaires, **22–23**
blood, **6–7**
body, **4–9**
bones, **4–5**
books, **28–29**
brain, **6**

cells, **4**

deepest dive, **16**
diving, **16**

egg, human, **4–5**

fastest person, **12–13**

fastest-selling digital
    single, **27**
fastest swimmer, **12**, **17**
films, **20–21**, **28**
free diving, **16**

hair, **8**, **19**
hands, **9**, **19**
heart, **6**
highest dive, **16**
highest-grossing film, **21**
highest jump, **14–15**

jumping, **14–15**

largest book, **28**
largest bookstore, **29**
largest film cast, **21**
largest hands, **9**
life expectancy, **10–11**
longest bones, **5**

longest cell, **4**
longest hair, **8**
longest jump, **14–15**
longest legs, **8**
longest mustache, **8**
longest nails, **8**
longest nose, **8**
longest swim, **17**
longest throw, **14–15**

marathon, **12–13**
most expensive work of
    art, **24–25**
most fingers and toes, **9**
most No. 1 albums, **26**
most prolific author,
    28–29
most successful
    recording artists,
    26–27

movies, **20–21**, **28**
muscles, **4–5**

oldest person, **10**
oldest work of art, **24**
organs, **6–7**

richest person, **22–23**

Shakespeare, William,
    28–29
shortest person, **9**
skin, **6**
smallest cell, **4**
sperm, **4–5**, **7**
strongest person, **18–19**
swimming strokes, **17**
systems, **6–7**

tallest person, **9**

weight lifting, **18–19**

First American edition published in 2016 by Lerner Publishing Group, Inc.

Copyright © 2015 by Wayland
published by arrangement with Wayland

Hungry Tomato™ is a trademark of Lerner Publishing Group, Inc.

All US rights reserved. No part of this book may be reproduced,
stored in a retrieval system, or transmitted in any form or by any
means—electronic, mechanical, photocopying, recording, or
otherwise—without the prior written permission of Lerner Publishing
Group, Inc., except for the inclusion of brief quotations in an
acknowledged review.

Hungry Tomato™
A division of Lerner Publishing Group, Inc.
241 First Avenue North
Minneapolis, MN 55401 USA

For reading levels and more information, look up this title at
www.lernerbooks.com.

Main body text set in Rockwell Std. Typeface provided by Monotype.

Library of Congress Cataloging-in-Publication Data

Richards, Jon, 1970–
    Record-breaking people / by Jon Richards and Ed Simkins.
        pages cm. — (Infographic top 10s)
        ISBN 978-1-4677-8596-9 (lb : alk. paper)
        ISBN 978-1-4677-9382-7 (pb : alk. paper)
        ISBN 978-1-4677-8647-8 (eb pdf)
        1. Curiosities and wonders—Juvenile literature. I. Simkins, Ed.
    II. Title.
    AG243.R37 2016
    030—dc23   2015002518

Manufactured in the United States of America
1 - BP - 7/15/15